A house in hue

By Omar Eby

 HERALD PRESS, SCOTTDALE, PENNSYLVANIA

Contents

1.

Death on Perfume River
(The Attack on the First Day)

A scream of artillery fire tore through the tropical silence of a muggy night. And through the restless sleep of June Sauder. The sound of war was not new to her but never had it fallen about so closely since her coming to Hue. Rarely did the muffled whine and thud among the distant hills press in for a conscious acknowledgment.

As June scrambled from her bed for the protection of the hallway she listened to the urgency of the strident voice of the incoming artillery. Instinctively she knew this would be something to reckon with.

It was four o'clock in the morning of January 31, 1968. The noise of yesterday's exploding firecrackers, proclaiming the beginning of Tet, the Vietnamese celebration of the Lunar New Year, was replaced by the explosion of war sounds. The house shuddered under the increasing blasts of artillery, whose fire punctured the darkness with great flashes of orange.

In the hallway June exchanged frightened whispers

with Harlan and Pauline Hochstetler, a young couple also with Vietnam Christian Service, the agency with whom June was associated. Though they lived at another house only a few blocks away, they had been encouraged to spend the night with June for security.

"It's close. Boy, it's close," Harlan said as they huddled together in the dark.

"Sounds as bad as the attack I lived through one night in Tam Ky," June replied, remembering the horror of a Viet Cong assault she had experienced a year earlier in another town.

When there seemed to be no lessening in the noise of attack, the three of them moved to a large walk-in closet off the hallway. It was the safest place in the house, away from the openings of windows and doors. They sat on the floor, waiting and listening, and not talking.

Dawn, with its first ashy light, was slow in coming. It was a long wait, almost more than they could endure. And little did they know then that those first long hours of waiting would fall the length of days. Of eight days.

At daybreak the attack had slackened in the streets outside June's house. She and the Hochstetlers went to the windows and carefully parted the drapes. Not anticipating the sight outside, they were stunned. Slipping quietly along the tree-lined street were

6

Vietnamese men in gray uniforms; others in common khaki shorts carried large packs strapped on their backs.

The three inside the house dropped the window drapes and stared at each other in disbelief.

"But . . . they're . . . they're not ARVN!" Harlan exclaimed.

And indeed the men stealing undisturbedly up the streets were not ARVN (Army of the Republic of Vietnam), for the ARVN had already begun a retreat from that section of Hue.

"They're either Viet Cong or North Vietnamese!" June said.

"What do we do?" Pauline asked, the fear in her voice slicing through the heavy stupor of the others.

They looked up at each other but only for a minute before turning away. The fear they saw in each other's eyes was too open, too naked. And it reflected too painfully their own fears.

"Well, let's keep quiet, for one thing."

"Do you think MACV knows?"

"Let's phone to warn them."

Now that the initial shock wore off their first reaction was to do something. Seeing the North Vietnamese running freely in the street was for June like watching armed robbers enter her neighbors' house. Everything within her cried out for her to take some action.

"Yes, do phone MACV," she urged Harlan.

7

They tried several times but could not make a telephone connection with MACV (Military Assistance Command, Vietnam)—fortunately, for they were to discover later that it could have been a mistake for their own safety.

There was nothing they could do. It would have been foolhardy to venture escape. Another look through the slit in the drapes underscored that. More North Vietnamese were scurrying along the street. The telephone service was out—but even so, if it weren't, whom really might they call for help? And at 7:30 o'clock the electricity went off. But not to do something—that, for aggressive, problem-solving-oriented Americans was even a greater anguish.

"I wonder how the guys are making out," June said, referring to the four Vietnam Christian Service fellows also assigned to the Hue unit. They lived in another small house a long Oriental suburban block away from June's house.

More than a year's experience of living in this war-torn country lay between June Sauder's arrival in Vietnam in late 1966 and the fury of the Tet offensive breaking over her head in Hue. As a trained home economist, June had spent earlier months in villages in Tam Ky and Di Linh, as well as the city of Saigon, before coming to Hue seven months ago.

June worked with the Vietnam Christian Service,

8

June Sauder

a relief and service agency created by the Mennonite
Central Committee, the Church World Service, and
the Lutheran World Relief to serve refugees and
other people in the emergency situation in Vietnam.
June, a Mennonite from Lancaster, Pennsylvania,
was sponsored by the Mennonite Central Committee,
which also administered the program in Vietnam for
the three cooperating agencies.

38 *Nguyen Hue—House of World Relief Commission office and home of June Sauder, where the seven stayed during the Tet offensive.*

In Hue, June was loaned to the World Relief Commission, which operated the Vocational Training Center in connection with the Evangelical Church of Vietnam. Here she served as an adviser in home economics instruction, as well as giving assistance at several of the refugee camps in the immediate vicinity.

At the same hour that morning of January 31, the other VNCSers—Paul Kennel, Jerry Sandoz, and

Kenneth Keefer—a block away, had dashed to the refrigerator when they were startled awake by the terrifying whistle of artillery shells going over their housetop. Since the house did not have a bunker, the fellows had decided that the safest place in their house during a mortar or artillery attack was near the refrigerator. It stood against heavy walls in an area providing the best protection from flying glass and shrapnel.

Also huddling in the darkness against the refrigerator with the three fellows was a colleague, Harley Kooker, visiting from the Dong Ha unit.

"Golly, something has really let loose!" Someone exclaimed under the wham of exploding artillery.

Another fellow chuckled, "Darn them VCs. Wakin' us up at this hour!"

Since nothing was hitting close to their house the four fellows decided to return to their bedroom and watch the fireworks through a window. The noise of mortar and artillery exploding and the increasing volleys of rifle fire was deafening.

"Man, I should be getting some real live war sounds," Kennel said. He dug out his tape recorder and set up the mike.

"That oughta impress 'em. When you get back home and play that to them."

At daybreak a sudden explosion just across the street at the television station brought the boys creeping to their bedroom window to peep out. Thick columns of smoke rose through the clean morning light. Even as the boys lay watching, another mortar struck another wall of a building at the TV station. And minutes later the home of a Vietnamese colonel took a direct hit.

"Well, there goes the electricity," Kennel said, as the recorder limped to a stop. It was 7:30 o'clock in the morning.

An hour and a half later, there was a lull in the fighting in the immediate vicinity of the boys' house. But they could hear that elsewhere across the city the attack had not slackened. About that time they saw two Americans walking down the street past their house and turning in at the TV station.

"Things have quieted down. Let's make a dash for June's house."

They all agreed. In high spirits they sprinted through the front door and clambered into the pickup truck, unaware that VC and NVA were in the streets.

June heard the truck jounce into the driveway outside her house. "Those stupid fellows. They'll get themselves killed," she cried, running to the door.

Through a partly opened door she waved urgently to the fellows still in the truck to come into the house immediately.

"Wow! How's that for war!" one said to her as he passed through the doorway.

12

"Get in here and shut up!" June snapped in an angry whisper.

"Don't get so excited. The attack's all over," another fellow responded expansively.

"Stop acting smart! There are VC and NVA all over the streets out there. We saw them," she added, gesturing to the Hochstetlers.

"Oooh! Go on, June! How could you tell they're VC?"

June was speechless with anger at the jocular attitude of the fellows. And for a moment she hated their foolish big-brotherliness toward her. You stupid fools, she thought, but finally found tongue to say: "Well, they were in uniforms . . . and not South Vietnamese army uniforms either."

"We know what we saw," the Hochstetlers came to her defense.

"I'll believe that when I see it."

"I just hope you live to see it!"

Tense with fear and smoldering with disgust, June turned away from the fellows as they threw themselves casually into chairs about the front room. Why trouble oneself with such impudence? June thought. Let them find out for themselves.

Not twenty minutes later the fellows saw for themselves North Vietnamese soldiers going by in the street—a sight which made the heart jump out of the chest. They watched in silence as the NVA in gray uniforms slipped along, their shoulder packs

13

camouflaged with branches of leaves. Others carried mortar tubes and dismounted machine guns.

A feeling of helplessness swept over the fellows and June as they watched the NVA stop at the house on the corner, set up a mortar launcher, and fire into the heart of the city. Other Vietnamese men in khaki shorts, presumably sympathizers of the VC, bundled supplies into the house. They were setting up a depot.

Strangely enough, someone had been preparing the house for months. The VNCSers had noticed a bunker being dug out, and more lately strands of barbed wire had been laced across it. Now suddenly the house was ready for use.

The high spirits, the loud laughter, the inane jokes dried instantly in the fellows watching all the activity across the street and reflecting upon its meaning.

"We're gonna be here for a while," Kennel said soberly.

Midmorning the city water went off, leaving the seven of them with a two-gallon filter tank full and a tray of ice. Around the same time fighting in the streets began picking up. The NVA entered the large Catholic monastery standing on another corner across the intersection of the streets. NVA were spotted moving about the power plant, located fifty feet from June's house. It apparently had been the target for much of the early-morning's attack. A continuous

14

booming filled the remainder of the morning.

The team tried eating a bit of lunch at noon only to find that gnawing apprehension had dulled their appetites. Later, as they sat about the living room, a stray bullet zipped through the window screen, passing between two of the fellows' heads. It splintered through the wooden doors of a cupboard and cut through several books before embedding itself in the wooden back of the case. They all ran for the protection of the hallway.

"And to think, only yesterday we were visiting friends and giving Tet greetings," June said. "And now this. It's so unreal."

The various members of the unit had spent yesterday, the first day of the Tet holidays, in various ways. Most had attended special services at the Vietnamese Protestant Church in Hue. Some had stayed for tea and cookies with the pastor's family. Others visited friends and employees, exchanging the traditional wishes for happiness, wealth, and longevity.

After a lunch at June's house, several put in a few hours of bookwork in the unit's office located in her house. Some watched television. Late afternoon they again visited with their Vietnamese friends.

In the afternoon one of the Americans from USAID dropped by to tell them that all the military personnel were on a 100 percent alert for the night. The team gave little thought to the report, for they had been clued in often before and nothing had happened. But when another American from the TV station came by later and repeated the same warning, they decided that the Hochstetlers should spend the night with June.

Midafternoon the first bombers swung low over the area of June's house, pounding the Provincial Headquarters which the NVA had overrun. A few of the fellows, curious and negligent, watched at the windows as the skyraiders dived to near treetop level before pulling up, a payload of death raining in their wake. When a large office window shattered from the blast of the exploding bombs, the curious watchers took some sane precautions. Later some choppers circled about at low altitudes, spraying the area with machine gun fire.

Dusk brought with it an ingeniously designed death-craft, dubbed "Puff." It was indeed a kind of mechanical magic dragon breathing fire. A DC-3 aircraft equipped with three mini-guns and a cannon, Puff was capable of firing thousands of rounds per minute, spraying an area 10 to 20 feet wide with bullets every few inches apart.

As night came on June hunted through the house for candles. Accustomed to regular electricity in Hue, she had few candles on hand, but enough to pro-

A gateway to the Citadel, the Imperial City in Hue.

17

vide some light. They closed the shutters and curtains but left the windows open so they could give and not break during the explosions. Mattresses were laid in the hallway, the large closet, and the bathroom, the zones of the house considered the most safe. And since there were more people than mattresses, most of the fellows made beds on the floor with chair cushions.

Night fell in the desolate streets of Hue, an ancient imperial city that the Vietnamese Buddhists regard as their religious capital. Across the Perfume River the Viet Cong proudly hoisted their red-and-blue flag over the nineteenth-century walled fortress known as the Citadel, a place which once served as the residence of Vietnamese emperors. On the other side of the river, seven Vietnam Christian Service workers repeated together the comforting words of the Twenty-third Psalm: "The Lord is my shepherd. . . . Thou art with me. . . . I shall dwell in the house of the Lord. . . ."

Did they even now dwell in a house of the Lord? June wondered.

All day it had been a house of ugly fear with each one of the team members reacting differently under the mounting tension. Some had talked too loudly, too boastfully. Some laughed too often in a strange highness. They had picked on each other, allowed sharp words of irritation, annoyed each other with sudden strange habits. One imitated all day too exactly the stutter of machine guns as they sounded in the streets.

Could her house of ugly fear become a house for her Lord? That too she would have to leave with Him. Tonight June found nothing but naked fear in the deepest recesses of her heart—where she had hoped to find courage.

2.

Richer by Tam Ky
(A Flashback to Earlier Experiences)

The airstrip at Tam Ky lies at a level spot isolated among the rice paddies. Westerners would not risk being dropped off there without the promise of immediate transport into town. This is Viet Cong territory. Doug Hostetter and Bill Herod met the small aircraft, for two additional staff were arriving from Saigon to flesh out their Vietnam Christian Service team.

To June Sauder, riding along in the pickup from the airstrip to the village, it was hard to believe the fellows' talk of gun and mortar fire on the edges of town. The pagan green rice paddies and the darkening mountains close by, even under the rain-laden skies, gave no hint of violence to her. After the months of living with the scream and thud of war being transported over Saigon's skies, and the congested profiteering in its streets, June felt the idyllic appeal of the quiet and green around Tam Ky.

"Just last evening I was shot at," Bill said. "I was

coming home a bit after dark when a warning shot with a command rang out. It turned out to be only a policeman. But it shows they're edgy."

Ahead of the truck rose the town, its thatch-roofed houses with an occasional one of stone strung along a main street of hard-packed sand, still moist from rainfall. A narrow-gauge railroad track lay rusting from disuse in the grass. Rice fields lapped right up to the backs of many houses.

Being among some of the first American women recently to be living in Tam Ky, June and Anne Falk, the other new VNCS arrivee, created a stir on their first afternoon's introductory visit about town. Wherever the team walked—to the USAID compound, to the small shops, to the Vietnamese restaurant —a crowd of children trailed them. With a mixture of curiosity and suspicion the adults stared at the smiling, self-conscious girls. June wondered what the villagers were thinking and how long it might take to change their blank stares to one of love—or hate.

Owned by USAID and loaned to VNCS till their own quarters—still in construction—were ready, the house made June uneasy. She felt it to be a mansion beside the thatched huts of the villagers; she was not sure that one built good relationships with a people by being so different.

Living without electricity, cooking on a small kero-sene stove, and sleeping on bamboo beds with straw mats helped to offset the first impressions of grandeur the house may have implied. Meals were taken in a small Vietnamese restaurant where one could join the local habit of tossing the bones from his meat dish to the floor for the dogs.

As hostess for the unit, June spent the first several days shopping for necessary items for the household, training a cook, and trying to get a modest routine established. She turned soon to the main task: What could she do in the town with any of the Vietnamese?

The two VNCS fellows were involved in community development work among the refugees. A refugee children's nutritional program, a bamboo handicraft project, English teaching, and local high school club activities filled their days.

"Do anything you can find to do in the field of your home economics training," June was told by her administrators in Saigon. Independent, on her own, responsible to no one, free to find the grass roots of any domestic science interests, and work from there up. The only one of the unit without an established organization to work with, she found such latitude was to prove discouraging frequently. During the first weeks she was told repeatedly by Tam Ky villagers that they had no need of her "foreign science."

"My area of work is new to the people of Tam Ky," June wrote at the end of her first month, "so things will have to move slowly until they have a better knowledge of what a home economist is and I understand their needs.

"This week I started spending some time at a day-care center for orphan children and children of laborers. I was asked to teach them embroidery. I also hope to do some work with them in the areas of art and recreation.

"This past week definite plans were laid to start a sewing class in one of the refugee camps. Students will be coming from several camps and the refugee office is providing the rooms and tables. I was asked also to teach home economics in the local elementary school and work with the possibility of getting girls started in 4T—Vietnam's equivalent to 4H—club activities."

Early in February, less than a month after the girls' arrival in Tam Ky, they were awakened shortly after midnight by a helicopter flying low over the house. Through the thickness of sleep, the girls were only half-aware that an announcement was being made in English from the helicopter. When the heavy silence of the night settled down over the town again and everything was quiet for another half hour they drifted off to sleep. Paul Longacre, then associate director of VNCS, was up from Saigon on a visit. He was asleep in an adjoining room. Doug and Bill were spending nights at a Catholic school across town.

Not ten minutes after everyone had again fallen asleep, hell let loose—or so it seemed, as they thrashed in their sleep to scramble under their beds. All around the house the staccato of rifles screamed with the artillery fire splitting the darkness with thunderous flashes.

After a few minutes of continuous barrage one imagines that it will soon end, but no pause comes and the frightening noise goes on and on, the house shuttering and the very floor seeming to heave under one. That the three of them should be huddled and shaking with fright on the floor was more than June had leisure to comprehend. For she, as with anyone under his first attack, was thinking of life itself.

"We'd better pray," Paul said. "There's not hope of getting outa here now." He had joined the girls, whose room was in a safer part of the house. While they could not be sure, they assumed from the noise outside that the Viet Cong had attacked a South Vietnam ammunition dump 100 yards from the back of their house.

The battle lasted for 45 minutes, then stopped as suddenly as it had begun. Again it was quiet, but to June, praying under her bed, it was no longer the idyllic quietness of a remote town in the lush tropics. It was a sinister silence, one never to be trusted again.

At four o'clock in the morning a loud rap and a command to open the door echoed through the house.

A too-common view—the U.S. Army.

It was a friend from the USAID compound with a guard, urging them to come to their compound for the rest of the night. "We're expecting another attack," the guard added, an unnecessary encouragement.

At dawn, the team returned to their house to find it safe except for a hole blown through the roof. All about them other houses showed damage, and 30 Vietnamese were killed. And when she learned that the houses of all the other Americans—the USAID, embassy, and army personnel—had been attacked and were heavily damaged, June stood inside her house with the golden light of an early morning falling through the open doorway, pondering the ways of life and death, of God and godlessness in that smitten land.

It was clear to her, as it was to the others on the team, that the Viet Cong had not wanted to harm any of them. Their house could have been destroyed but the Viet Cong had not touched it. Why were they spared? June wondered.

"I can now say I truly know what it is like to be in the middle of actual fighting," she wrote to her parents. "It is a very frightening experience and one I am glad I lived through just for the knowledge of what the Vietnamese must live with."

With June's constant push against village inertia, a few projects gave the appearance of taking some shape. After spending some days observing classes at a kindergarten for orphans and children of laborers, she made a three-month outline of what she hoped to do with the help of the teacher in the areas of art, crafts, and recreation. Acquaintance with this teacher led to an exchange of language instruction, with June teaching the Vietnamese teacher English in return for tutoring in Vietnamese.

Plans for sewing classes at one of the refugee camps got snagged in the bureaucracy of the refugee office. But at the Tu Hiep Camp the first 10-week experiment class of 10 students, ages 15-20, got under way. Schemes for additional programs in personal hygiene and health were destined to remain intact on paper, shattered in hopes.

So too were the hopes to do work with the 4T club in small gardens, nutrition, child care, and personal hygiene. June had collected 14 shy Vietnamese girls together in a hamlet outside Tam Ky and formed a 4T club.

It had been hard work getting 14 teenage girls together, for the community was conservative and its girls were not to be easily entrusted with these strange American women newly come to town. As for the callers at her house, June found that most of them were men or small children.

June and Anne mostly biked along the dirt roads and paths to and from their many points of growing contacts. It was not uncommon to have children throw stones at them, expressing in their childish way the cold, suspicious stares of their mothers. This was true of one particular area of the town. The suspicion and small hostilities of the children troubled June. She hoped for a way into their midst.

It came one afternoon when one of the 4T girls invited June to her house. She received little from the mother except a stare of curiosity and fear, but the children soon clustered about her, inquisitive and friendly.

"And the very next day, there was no more stone-throwing when I went pedaling through that area," June commented to her team.

The kindergarten teacher also invited June to visit her home. She was warmly received by the mother, and saw here the possibility of an opening to find out about Vietnamese family life, food habits, and customs of Tam Ky.

"My getting into homes is rather slow, but I feel I need a warm welcome before entering and asking any questions," June wrote.

While the visits to Vietnamese homes were rare for the girls during these first months, visits to their American house by the town's curious, particularly the teenagers, were constant. If at first it was something novel to be eating one's dinner and cleaning the house with one's neighbors peering in at all the windows, June and Anne soon found that they were going to have to honor their usual need for privacy if they were to keep sane.

One Saturday in particular they had such a growing crowd of visitors that the girls found the situation getting slightly out of hand.

"They are so curious and do about as they please and even go anywhere through the house without asking," June complained to Doug, hopeful for some insight from him who had spent a longer time in Tam Ky. "It seems as if they have an idea that our place is public property."

Sunday offered no relief from the press of visitors, though for the first time the girls kept all the windows and doors closed and refused to see anyone.

"After yesterday's crush of visitors with all our conversation in Vietnamese and that alone very tiring when one has a limited vocabulary and not fully acquainted with the Tam Ky accent, Anne and I could not face the idea of attending the Vietnamese church service where we cannot understand a thing, nor could we face one more visitor," June wrote to her mother that morning, perhaps as an attempt to explain to herself the frustration she found mounting in her. "When several visitors impolitely insisted on coming in I wanted to scream!"

After talking the situation over with Doug, Anne and June decided that they simply had to have occasional privacy. Since their Vietnamese friends did not understand this need or failed to respect it, they further felt that closing the house with themselves inside would at least be a temporary answer.

Monday morning they started a campaign of getting the children to play away from the windows and doors of the house. At first the children did not cooperate but when they found that these Americans could also be firm, they began to listen. Through all of this June found it hard to know how firm to be and still keep an atmosphere for nurturing good relationships.

Fifteen miles east of Tam Ky a large marine base lay at the coastal village of Chu Lai. Doug and June set out on the motor scooter to visit the dentist at this base. Some weeks earlier, June had chipped a tooth which was now throbbing for attention. The day away from her work at Tam Ky was a welcome excursion, and her letter to her family written some days later still held some of the lift in spirits she had experienced.

"We took the scooter and headed down Highway 1. The countryside is beautiful. And now that the rainy season is over, all the fields are a bright green under the tropical sun. About a mile out of Tam Ky we came upon some marines who were using a grader to improve the road.

"They could not believe their eyes and asked if we were French or Americans. They asked all the usual questions of where we were going and why and what we were doing in Vietnam.

31

"They warned us that the road gets much worse several miles down further towards the coast. They did not think we could make it. But we decided to investigate and started off again.

"We had not gone far when Doug lost control of the scooter and I took a slow flip backward off the scooter into the five-inch mud. I came up with a big red mud spot on the back of my white blouse and skirt. The mud simply oozed over the tops of my shoes. I thought it all rather funny.

"We decided to go on and came to a place where the mud was eight inches deep. I got off the scooter and sank to my ankles. By this time one of the large army trucks was coming along, and one of the marines we had just talked to was in the truck. They stopped and took me along in the truck while Doug struggled with the scooter.

"We met at a small village just outside the large marine base. From there on we had paved road.

"The base must cover 10 square miles along the beautiful seacoast. The dental office is located along this shore and I could enjoy the salty breeze and the lapping of the surf while on the dentist's chair. The dentist was very nice and we had a great discussion about the war and our relations with the Vietnamese people.

"Since it was noon, we took dinner at the officers' mess hall. It was a delicious American meal of meat loaf, potatoes, pickles, red beets, carrots, tea, pineapple upside-down cake, and homemade bread. The dentist invited us to return some Sunday for a charcoal steak dinner along the beach. We just might take him up on that sometime!"

For some weeks the Saigon administration of VNCS was receiving reports about the growing lack of security in the Tam Ky area. While the unit itself tried to keep alert to such rumors, they did not feel in any greater danger since that one shattering experience some weeks earlier. So it came as some surprise to the Tam Ky unit to receive a message from Saigon that June and Anne were to leave immediately for Saigon. Having to leave the town just when she was beginning to get some handles for working at home economics, June was discouraged with the setbacks this would cause in her work.

In less than three months, June, with Anne, was making the trip to airstrip, believing she could return to Tam Ky in a few weeks, a few months at the most. Even while she worked in the Saigon office she laid plans for her work in Tam Ky: securing two Vietnamese cadres to help as her counterparts in home economics. But June was never to return to Tam Ky.

3.

Watchers at the Windows
(*The Siege Begins the Second Day*)

The early morning was quiet, the streets of the city strangely empty. The seven VNCSers inside their house were caught in the same silent web. Everyone—everything seemed to be waiting. Watching, listening, and waiting.

A distant shutter of guns, a sparrow chirping in the courtyard, the muffled tread of some passersby on the street. And with slow, heavy motions, the morning began moving, after what seemed to be hours of being caught in an inexplicable freeze.

Paul went to the window and parted the drapes a slit. His eyes fell immediately on a small cluster of gray-clad North Vietnamese.

"Look!" His whispered command was tight with disbelief. It brought the others scuttling to the window, crowding for a view through the crack.

The NVA were marching two Americans in civilian dress down the street across the intersection at the power plant.

"It's. . . ." Paul didn't have to name the Americans. The unit knew them personally—two friends from the USAID office.

The effect of seeing the Americans, with arms tied behind them, being led off down the street and out of sight was a profound shock to the watchers behind the curtains. Their minds staggered with disbelief, making them blink and take a second look. Each fought to find the courage to admit what his eyes were following. And none of them dared search for the words to say how badly he was frightened.

It was a solemn group who turned away from the windows and went about picking up and handling the nothings of the morning as they waited. Outside the house, the rumble and bursts of war gathered momentum, as though once the shuffling noise of the opening overture of captured Americans being led away was finally played through, the real dissonance of war could be let loose. More North Vietnamese were running in the streets in front of June's house and the burst of small-arms fire told that they were occasionally spotting South Vietnamese Rangers.

It was a long morning, a time for long thoughts. And June's mind went back to the time of her arrival in Hue, more than six months ago. While she was looking forward to her new assignment in Hue she also had to fight again that rising feeling of not wanting to go anywhere. It was not the tense

At the Vocational Training Center, classes were also held in carpentry and mechanics.

atmosphere of Hue she fought. The VNCS team had packed suitcases on minutes' notice for evacuation several times in the past, though no one had evacuated during the past ten months. Such insecurity she felt she could live with—Tam Ky having been her tutor.

Rather, it was the feeling of just wanting to rest in the routines of something stable and familiar. But once in the air again, with the noise and dirt of Saigon behind her, she found strength for the expected demands.

She was assigned as an adviser to the Vocational Training Center operated by World Relief Commission in connection with the Evangelical Church of Vietnam. On her arrival, June found about 120 students with a second-grade education. Classes were held in home economics, literacy, carpentry, agriculture, hatmaking, basketmaking, religion, mechanics, blockmaking, and history of Vietnam. Besides the more formal studies, the center operated a farm for raising pigs, chickens, and cows.

In home economics she found them teaching child care, sewing, cooking, health, home improvement, and other short courses. The home economics course was a short one of two months, after which those students who desired could enroll in a more advanced class.

June had a few days in which to learn the ropes from a Mrs. Milk, who was leaving Vietnam with her husband. Honored to have been given the assignment, June was not without some concern about her inexperience in light of the fairly heavy demands of the schedule.

"I would find it much easier to do the teaching myself than to help guide and train the teachers," she wrote at that time.

She was soon in the thick of it, with no two days alike. Being the only American home economist in the upper provinces of South Vietnam, June was frequently expected to observe and advise projects in other villages, which caused shuffling of schedules. Even life at the vocational school with its attempts at routine was not infrequently disrupted with rather bizzare happenings.

Once while June was sitting in on one of the general home economics classes, a workman entered and proceeded to paint the first-aid cabinet right in the middle of the classroom. She debated whether to ask him to leave, since he was disturbing the class, but decided against it since an interpreter was not present to explain carefully. Later, she noticed that he was painting a red cross on the front of the cabinet, which would have been expected, but to her horror, June saw that he was making the Christian cross instead of the first-aid cross. This was too much, so she stopped everything, explained his error, got him to correct it, and then went on with the class.

A refugee at the Relief Training Center instructs a student in hat-making.

Another morning June was sitting in on an advanced sewing class when all of a sudden the literacy teacher came to the window and started teasing and flirting with the sewing instructress. June thought the fellow was supposed to be teaching his literacy class, at least not disturbing another class. She went to investigate.

"My students are practicing their writing. They don't need me in the room then," he explained.

The sudden scream of jets flying at treetop level broke through June's thoughts. She with the other six threw herself facedown on the floor. There was no bombing, but the noise seemed enough to flatten the house on them. Never had any of them experienced such a helpless feeling of lying there not knowing what was going to happen.

At noon they picked up a news report on a portable radio. The Far East Broadcasting Co., Philippines, reported that three companies of marines had entered Hue and had routed the Viet Cong. But with all the strafing and bombing taking place down by the Perfume River and the North Vietnamese running in the streets, the unit found the news a little hard to believe.

"We'd better open up the bunker," someone suggested. "We might be needing it before this is over."

The house, built by the French, had an underground bomb shelter. Under the floor of the hallway a ten-foot by five-foot bunker had been dug out at the time of the construction of the house. It had a two-foot cement top.

The bunker had not been opened for some years. After heaving off the top, the fellows had shone a

41

flashlight into the hole. It was dark and dank and their light showed that the floor was covered with water.

"Oooh! I'll never go down into that hole," the girls chorused, shuddering at the prospects.

"But we could use some of that water," June said, recovering her senses.

The city water had gone off early the day before. They had not thought to store water. By the evening of today they would be out of the last drinking water. They had not washed and the commode needed flushing.

Whether or not the water would really be needed, the unit did not know, of course, but they took the sane precaution to scoop it out and store it in containers. Some was used for flushing the toilet. But the most was strained and boiled. It looked like old tea but had none of the aroma. For coffee and cooking the color hardly mattered. As for drinking, the ration of a few swallows per person was later to become a welcome beverage.

The afternoon passed more quickly than had the morning. The bunker preparation with scooping four inches of water out had provided diversionary relief. When gray shadows began to gather in the corner of the house with evening coming on, they lowered chairs into the bunker for possible use during the night.

With supper over and the electricity still off and

some feeling of needing to preserve the few candles for possible urgencies, there was little incentive for the seven, after spending the past two days together, to sit up in the dark any longer.

"Yea, though I walk through the valley of the shadow of death. . . ." Again they quoted the Twenty-third Psalm together and tried to pray before going to bed.

They sat in a circle about the room, the candles weaving their strange magic of warmth and intimacy, the shatter of artillery across town so alien to the quietness in the house. It was not obvious just what they should pray for. Might they ask for their own protection when the sound of death rained about them on their neighbors? That their parents and friends should not worry about them? That they, the whole lot of them Christian pacifists—would soon be evacuated by the marines? That the lives of their Vietnamese co-workers might be spared?

They thanked God for the protection of the day and humbly asked Him for the same for their Vietnamese friends and themselves during the long night.

June lay on her mattress on the bathroom floor. During the early part of the night, waiting for the gift of sleep, she thought of her work at the vocational center. She enjoyed the advisory position, finding it interesting to work directly with the Vietnamese teachers. She was pleased at the trust they showed in her, though it had not been easy at first. Being younger or at least near the same age as most of the Vietnamese teachers, June was not always respected. "I am still trying to find the balance between being a friend and an adviser so that what I say is taken seriously and not just in fun," she once wrote. And to be taken seriously, June went about her work with an air of determination.

During the first weeks of acquainting herself with the nature of her work and sources of assistance, she visited refugee centers and domestic science clubs in other villages. About one such day's activities she had written to her mother.

"Wednesday afternoon I went to Hoa Luon Refugee Camp near the school with Co Tuyen. She is a Vietnamese home extension worker and was calling on one of her Home Improvement Clubs. She said the meeting would start at three o'clock, but as usual in Vietnam when we arrived the place was empty. They didn't even have the benches or stove in the room for the class.

"We drove through the camp honking the horn and then some women began arriving. It was four o'clock before the meeting started. Co Tuyen was showing them how to make a cake using a root vegetable and how to bake it by placing it on top of a kerosene burner, covering the pan with a lid and placing hot charcoals on top. It worked nicely.

"The next morning I took my general home economics teacher to the same camp to see the cement slabs for washing clothes which they had constructed, and the improved stove they were using."

About another day's activities June had written: "Wednesday was a busy day and I was so worn out I could hardly eat or sleep. I went to school in the morning as usual and at noontime could not get a siesta because people were calling at the house all that time.

"At two o'clock I left for the Agriculture Services Offices where I met Co Tuyen to go with her to the Achievement Day in a village about 20 miles from Hue; they were closing their sewing classes in 4T. Tom and another fellow USAID also drove up.

"What a drive! To start with, my car has a broken spring and I had to take more girls than I thought best. But that was not the worst. The road is in terrible condition. I have never seen such ruts in my life. We crossed makeshift bridges and one railroad bridge where my tires kept getting caught between the rails.

"The worst came when we turned off the highway and onto a dirt road. When we neared the village we had to cross an irrigation ditch which was just wide enough for my car.

"Fortunately we had to wait another hour before the program began. I was simply worn out. It gave

45

me time to talk to the children and see what they were doing. They then gave a program which included sewing demonstrations, singing, folk dances, speeches, and presentation of awards.

"By then it was five o'clock and we Americans were getting a little concerned about security way out there in VC territory. We were finally able to get the school girls hustled back into the car and head for Hue. This time Tom drove my car for me and we made better time.

"I got back at 6:15, showered, ate a bite, and by seven was in my classroom teaching English. I think you understand now why I say I was too tired to eat or sleep. But it has all been most interesting."

This was not the first reference to Tom which June made in her letters. She had first met him on the Saigon-to-Danang leg of her flight into Hue. They had talked about Vietnam, Vietnam Christian Service, and the Mennonites. Tom, a Christian agriculturist, newly arrived for USAID, had not known where he would be assigned. He took June's address and telephone number, saying he would probably see her sometime during his stay in Vietnam.

Not four days later at a banquet in Hue, the city to which he was also assigned, Tom made inquiry of June's whereabouts. Over the months the two found delight in each other's presence, June beginning to lose a battle with Cupid.

Sleep did not come easy to the unit the second

46

June Sauder in traditional Vietnamese dress, with two co-workers at the Refugee Training Center.

night of the siege. But when the mind did close out, the scream of incoming artillery rent the night and they scrambled through the dark house for the protection of the bunker.

Most of that second night was spent getting in and out of the bunker. For June it seemed a night of fear without end: "Though I walk through the valley of the shadow of death, I fear no evil; for thou art with me. . . ." She cried out in her heart to know the presence of those words. And to lay at rest her fears . . . of her own death . . . of her Vietnamese co-workers . . . of Tom.

47

4.

A Sabbath of No Rest
(The Third, Fourth, and Fifth Days)

Shortly after breakfast on the third day of their siege, the team heard a heavy vehicle growling down the street. An American military truck with two marines lumbered into view. The team watched in frozen horror, knowing what would happen. The NVA at their supply house on the corner let the truck get halfway to the power plant where other NVA waited. Then both positions opened up with machine guns, catching the truck in a crossfire, killing both marines. One fellow tumbled limply from the truck as it coasted crazily out of sight around the corner of the plant.

Trembling with fear, June turned from the window. She was aware that she was actually shaking, almost uncontrollably, and realized she'd have to do something to hang on. She'd cook them a big lunch for a change.

"For lunch I'm going to make fried chicken and mince pie," she announced to the others, a strained brightness in her voice.

"But it's too early to start dinner," Pauline objected.

"Yeah, we've only just had breakfast."

"I sure don't get hungry waiting around like this."

Indeed, it was too early to start preparing lunch, June realized, and on sudden impulse replied. "But first I'm going to cut out a dress."

To pass the time and keep the mind away from the gnawing fear of the unknown, some read books and old magazines, others played Rook and solitaire, while Pauline copied recipes from cookbooks and June cut out a dress.

As she laid out the pattern on the fresh stiff cloth, June wondered about her Vietnamese colleagues at the Training Center and the other employees at the farm, seven kilometers outside the city. Had they been killed, the farm plundered? Or had the Viet Cong again made only a routine checkup, as they did occasionally at the refugee centers at night?

A few months before Tet June had written about one such visit: "The Viet Cong, numerous in this area, have been visiting our camps frequently at night during the past months. Last week they tied up the night watchman, interrogating him. To their question of whom he worked for, he replied, 'The Lord.' They released him, doing him nor the school any harm.

50

A refugee camp in Vietnam.

"One wonders how long we can continue to receive such good treatment from the VC. It's late October and we're just coming into the rainy season when attacks are often more frequent. I suppose we would leave at the request of the American government but please don't worry about us. We are happy with our work and plan to stay as long as possible."

A growing sense of unity between the Americans and the Vietnamese staff at the Training Center was one of several lifts June experienced in the recent months.

When she first arrived at her Hue assignment she noted some suspicion and lack of respect from the Vietnamese teachers whom she was to advise in home economics. Mostly, she felt, it was a matter of age, for in the Orient, with its deep reverence for older people, she was looked upon as being too young to be of much help.

"When one is working under such a situation," June wrote, "we Americans have to learn to lose ourselves in their problems. To forget that we are Americans and try to see through their eyes the life they face."

All that her Vietnamese partners needed many times was a bit of encouragement to talk. "Faculty meetings were quite a blessing because there was great freedom to express feelings and work together through problems of running the Center.

"In a number of our non-Christian assistants I

noticed that they were beginning to sense we were working together for more than a handout. They began to understand that the World Relief Commission team and national Christians at the Center were genuinely concerned with what was happening to the Vietnamese people because of the war."

The interpreter at the Center had expressed this to her one time. "I hated Americans but now I see that you are different, that you are in Vietnam for a different cause."

After the Vietnamese discovered that June and the other VNCSers were not there to quiz them about their political beliefs but to do everything within their power to help them, they relaxed considerably. So much so that they were no longer hesitant about being seen in the villages in the company of VNCS members.

"I was thrilled last November when two of the home economics teachers took me with them for a whole morning. They asked me to wear Vietnamese dress and accompany them to celebrate some national day.

"We went to their homes to visit with their families, dropped by the Perfume River to watch boat races, and then strolled through a park. I was amazed that they weren't afraid to be seen with an American.

"I have a limited knowledge of the language and could not understand everything they were saying.

53

June Sauder with two of her Vietnamese friends.

But during the past few months we had grown that close to each other that we could communicate beyond words. They wanted me as a friend and I desperately wanted them as friends."

June kept her word and served up a dinner of fried chicken, cucumber salad, and mincemeat pie. While the lack of electricity created no problem for cooking—she had a gas stove—meat in the freezing compartment of the electric refrigerator had thawed. When June's cook came in to check on the house, they gave her some meat to share with their Vietnamese neighbors before it spoiled.

Chi Hai, June's cook, burst into tears when she saw the seven VNCSers still in the house. She was wishing that they had left a few days earlier to attend the VNCS conference in Dalat.

"It's not safe here. You'll get killed," she cried.

The team tried to reassure her that while they were aware of the danger there was little they could do about it now.

"God is watching over us," June added.

In the afternoon the team killed time by sweeping the whole house, washing all the dirty dishes which had accumulated, and boiling more of the water which had been scooped from the basement. It was the last time they wasted water on washing dishes. From then on they merely wiped them out and returned them to the table for the next meal. They made name tags to mark the place where each of the seven sat, so each would at least use his own unwashed dishes. Drinking water was rationed to a few swallows a day.

The midafternoon calm was slit wide open with the screech of two F-8 Crusader jets streaking down the street at treetop height. The girls screamed and ran for the bunker. The fellows ran to the living room to watch out the windows.

The jets strafed the ARVN compound in which the NVA had set up an antiaircraft gun. It was a fantastic air display for the fellows watching. The jets dipped and whirled to return, their 20mm cannons firing round after round of eight-inch-long shells. Just as suddenly they spiraled away, the NVA antiaircraft gun in the ARVN compound silenced. Later, the watchers at the window saw ARVN soldiers carrying a South Vietnamese flag move up the street toward their compound.

That evening the team heard the news on the small transistor radio which June's cook had brought them during one of her visits. "Jets from Danang were called in to attack an ARVN compound overrun by VCs. It was a successful mission," the newscaster reported. It was also an odd experience for the VNCSers to be told by an impersonal voice only hours later what they had witnessed earlier in the afternoon.

°   °   °

Saturday, the fourth day of waiting, was quiet. Only sporadic bursts of small-arms fire broke the strange lull. Even the night had been mute, a bullet through the office window splintering the silence only fragmentarily.

As June watched at the window she saw people —Vietnamese civilians—venture into the streets in numbers greater than any time since the attack. And on the bright morning the shouts of children at play came to her ears. A distant peal of church bells fell tremulously about her. God, is it over? she prayed, hopefully. Can we go back to our work? Or get out of here?

Kennel joined her at the window just as two American military men walked into view on the way from their house to the TV station, which they operated.

"If it's that safe, maybe we can slip over to our house to pick up some food and water," Kennel said.

If they were to stay many more days besieged in June's house the seven would need more food. Water was already badly needed. Some of the other fellows joined Kennel in wanting to make a break for their house. But June wasn't convinced of the wisdom of the risk. At least not at first.

"You don't know if it is safe or not," she replied.

"We'll be gone for two minutes," Keefer said.

"There haven't been any NVA down at that corner post all morning," Kooker added.

57

Not only did the fellows want to brave it for the food and water but they were curious to see what might have happened over at their house. And sitting for more than three days and nights in a house had really got to them. They simply needed to get out, and were willing to take the risk.

So Paul Kennel, Ken Keefer, and Harley Kooker slipped out the door, stole along a fence, and then sprinted across the open street. They dropped down an alley, keeping close to walls before jumping over a fence into their own courtyard.

Their house had taken a near hit from artillery. Shrapnel was scattered about the driveway, the trunk of a coconut palm slashed in half. The doors hung open, and for a moment the boys were not sure what they might find. The house was a mess. Plaster from the ceilings and some walls covered the tables and beds and floors. Splinters of glass from all the broken windows lay strewn among the plaster. Holes gaped in the roof. Fortunately, ten 55-gallon barrels of gasoline stored in the adjacent garage had not been struck.

Quickly they gathered up water, tinned food, two cases of C-Ration (military field operations rations), cameras, and a few handbags of clothing Kooker had brought with him on his visit. Outside their house again they met the two Americans returning from the TV station, who warned them to get in their house. It might be quiet today but NVA still occupied the area. The fellows hurried back safely to June's house.

Lunch was being served when the twelve o'clock news on the transistor radio told of the VC slaying of the six Christian and Missionary Alliance missionaries at Banmethuot. Like the scene of a stilled frame of a movie, the listeners were frozen immovable in an ice slab of fear. Seldom have the living listened with such foreboding to an account of the dying.

It was a tremendous blow to June. She sat down weakly in a chair, her hunger wiped out. Fear filled her stomach, then spilled over to rise in suffocating waves. The news was a reminder to her that perhaps she and her friends would not be safe for long now. The room was silent when the news ended. And no one broke that silence as a few of them tried to eat the lunch waiting before them.

Fear had done strange things to June during the previous days. It dulled the appetite and made it possible to do with less food. It heightened her senses, particularly her hearing, so that it seemed as though she heard more, that she heard sounds of people or things moving toward her but never really arriving. And while fear made her very alert it also made her very tired, so that in the evening she was exhausted, though having done nothing all day but sitting and waiting.

But with the news of the slain missionaries fear

Refugee children eating CSM—a high protein powder made of corn, soya, and milk. June Sauder conducted a study to discover precisely what nutritional effects the CSM had on the children in the refugee camps.

swelled within June until it burst. Great waves of a strange calmness, cozily comfortable, folded over her. She was sinking into a great blanket of torpidity.

She felt she would probably not get through another day alive and wished that whoever they were, would come now, today, and put an end to her life.

Later, June was nearly unable to explain how fear could evolve to such calmness nor how she lived through the following days with such smothering apathy. She cared little if she'd ever be able to pick up her work, even on one of the most interesting projects: a CSM nutritional study in the villages around the Center.

CSM is a high protein powder made of corn, soya, and milk which was used in the feeding programs at the refugee camps. Cooked in water for a few minutes, it was easily prepared with the crudest of kitchen equipment. June's study was to discover precisely what nutritional effects the CSM had on the children in the refugee camps. It called for study of the Vietnamese regular diet at the camp and its nutritional value. The assignment demanded the best of diplomacy—to go nosing into what people eat.

"I hired two girls and a young man to help me make the study," June wrote of the project. "I could have done it myself but felt that the Vietnamese ought to. For one thing, these three young people were from the Evangelical Christian Church, which needed to be challenged into helping other people about them."

June prepared a simple questionnaire for her assistants to use. Her strategy was to first call on the village chief for his ideas, asking him if he thought it a good plan to make such a study. When he agreed, she asked him to introduce her team to the refugee village.

"He would go around and tell everyone that we were coming, that we wanted some information which would help them. Thus, we were able to ask questions about their food and get some ideas as to what their nutritional problems were."

Not everything went smoothly, however. An interpreter quit and a new one had to be secured. Local elections proved distracting. Then a VC attack in the area caused further confusion. Finally, some weeks later, June was able to set up the experiment.

"In the one village I gave the children CSM. In the other village I gave no supplemental food to the children's diet. The first day we weighed and measured the children, and will do this every week. We are feeding a total of 88 children between the ages of six months and eight years.

"I hired two people from the refugee village to prepare the food. I could have gone in and done it myself but it is more important that they help their own people. So we taught them how to do it and why all the record-keeping was important. I found that so often our programs fail because we don't explain in detail why we are doing something or in what way it will help them. We don't allow them time to ask their questions.

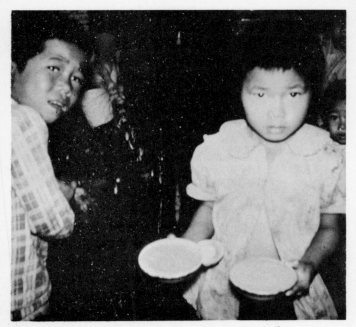

Refugee children receiving CSM mixture (corn, soya, milk).

"I stayed with the Vietnamese assistants for three days, answering questions of the mothers, who were curious but reserved about the experiment," June wrote.

Other villages soon heard about the experiment and wanted to cash in on the program in some way. But at that time, June couldn't guarantee them anything, attempting to explain what an experiment was.

When the experiment ended, they discovered that

June Sauder, at Refugee Training Center, preparing for blanket distribution. The quilts were made by sewing circles in the U.S.

64

the children in the refugee village receiving the CSM supplemental food gained three times more in a ten-week period than the children who did not receive it. The information spread rapidly from village to village, and not by a massive propaganda assault, but naturally—mothers swapping gossip at the wash blocks or in the rice fields or on the footpaths.

By Sunday, the fifth day of the siege, life was taking on a pattern for June. The first thing she did each morning she awoke was to check who was moving in the streets.

After a day and a night of little activity in which she had not seen one NVA in the streets or at the supply house on the corner, it was bitterly dismaying to find the NVA back at their posts. A sense of futility swept through her, a feeling she had not tasted since a blanket distribution incident a few months earlier.

With other VNCSers she had worked hard in getting blankets ready to give out in all the nearby villages, particularly the refugee villages. Many old-fashioned, hand-knotted quilts were among the blankets. June knew that her own Mennonite people had helped stitch and knot many of these same quilts which she would be giving out.

"I thought of the hours and hours the ladies had spent back in the States preparing these quilts. I thought of all that they must have talked about as they knotted threads. As I was helping with the distribution in the villages, I was impressed with the fact that I was somehow sharing with somebody back home who cared. While I had the thrill to actually place the thick comforter in the arms of a needy Vietnamese, I was really only just another hand in a long chain of extended, compassionate hands."

That evening as she drove her car back to Hue she saw a village chief pedaling his bike along the road leading into the city. Strapped on the carrier were three newly distributed blankets. June knew only too well what the old man had in mind. He was going to sell them.

"They're a thankless bunch of robbers," June stormed to Kennel when she flopped down in the unit's office. "I am so tired of trying to help people who show no appreciation. I . . . I just give up!"

"But I just came from giving blankets and comforters in a village where people were genuinely thankful," Kennel chided.

"I know . . . I know . . . ," June said wearily.

"But didn't anyone's face or eyes light up with appreciation? Aren't you condemning a whole group of people just because one or two did something wrong?"

In her better moments June knew that Kennel was right but that night she was too exhausted and blue to admit his truth. And it was not the only time that her gift for realistic appraisal of life and people and situations carried an all-too-well earned conclusion which hinted at pessimism. One year after being in Vietnam she had written to her mother:

"The week has been the usual scramble. My car now has to be pushed to be started. The oven control is broken and I can't use the oven. The salt water rusts the pipes which stains the water which is going to ruin my clothes. And yesterday the cook rolled the molasses crinkles in salt instead of sugar.

"As I sit and think back it seems impossible that one year of my term is already past. Sometimes it is even hard to realize that I am in another country. I feel I have learned much and am learning much about myself. I am happy and do enjoy my term but am also looking forward to coming home. I think I will never be able to fit back into the mold of our home community again. Maybe I have become too liberal. This can be both good and bad. Working in a situation such as this makes so many things seem unnecessary and sheds new light on things one always thought were so right or wrong.

"Sometimes we have difficult decisions to make concerning our position here—what we are trying to do, what friends to associate with, might one date a soldier?

"I miss having an English language church to attend, and am disappointed with the Christian church here. It is one-dimensional, emphasizing salvation, without deep concern for a witness to the social order. However, the church has a capacity to suffer which few North American Christians know anything about.

"So much for the summary of my first year in Vietnam."

While June stood carefully watching at the window and reflecting on the depression of earlier months, she saw about 100 people coming down the street. Nurses and medics were among them. She concluded that the NVA were releasing the staff and patients and refugees who were caught at the hospital when the city was seized.

Sunday saw some of the heaviest fighting in the area of the VNCS house. Much of the day was spent crawling in and out of or huddling in the dank bunker. For hours it seemed to June that one burst of artillery fire followed another.

Their VNCS warehouse across the street was struck. The neighbor's house was blown apart. The Catholic school and power plant were taking a pounding, all presumably from American or ARVN forces, for these two places were occupied by the NVA, as well as the ARVN compound itself.

As they sat in the bunker, the team could hear the thud of artillery landing about the house. Kennel counted the rounds. Twenty-seven fell in the block, twelve landed about the house, some as close as a foot from its walls. Though none hit the house directly, much of the glass in the windows was smashed.

The six o'clock news said that sixteen U.S. military men had been killed and forty-four wounded, that fourteen Vietnamese civilians were injured. But June and her colleagues doubted that such a report was true. For as heavy as the battle was just in their area of Hue—and during lulls they could hear heavy bombing in the direction of the Citadel—it was impossible to believe that no Vietnamese civilians were killed. Before they had fled to their bunker, they had seen women and children and old men running both directions in the street, some toward town and some away from the center of town. Many were already refugees without homes who had crowded into the city from the hamlets for security. They would have been helpless before the impersonal machines raining hell on them.

All through Sunday night, to a background of screaming artillery tearing the fabric of the rain-laden blackness, June and the other six hustled from their beds on the floors to the hard chairs in the bunker. The Sabbath had not been a day of rest. Nor the night of the Sabbath.

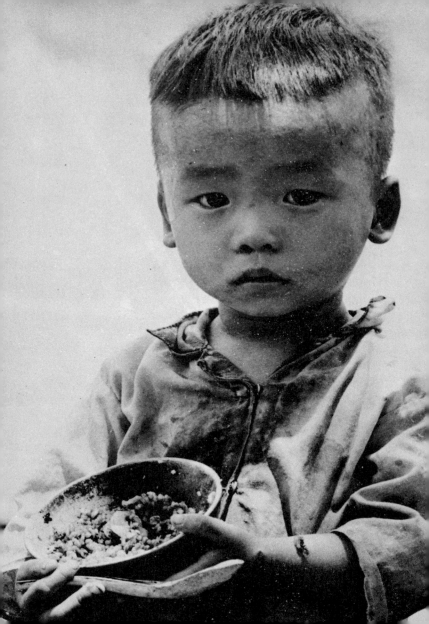

5.

Sweet Fear of Death
(The Sixth, Seventh, and Eighth Days)

The quiet morning of the sixth day—Monday, February 5—again caused false hopes to rise. Perhaps it was all over. But as the VNCSers looked out the window toward Nguyen Hue Street they could see the NVA moving about at the house on the corner or dog-trotting up the street. The view was depressing but by now the situation had become dreamlike for all the members of the unit. Nothing seemed to shock them anymore.

"How's the food supply?"

"We're going to have to start rationing food and water harder," June said.

"Should probably eat just twice a day."

"Yes, eating at about eleven and six o'clock."

"And cutting our drinking water down to three swallows per day."

No one complained nor cheated. They all understood the necessity of the stricter precaution.

Chi Hai, June's cook, came to the kitchen window

71

to warn the team not to even step outside the house today. Previously they had occasionally gone out on a covered breezeway in the rear of the house which connected the kitchen with the servants' quarters.

"The NVA are all around the house," Chi Hai warned. "They're not just in the streets. You must stay inside."

It was a bit of a hardship for some of the fellows. They had thought the breezeway a protected-enough place occasionally to sneak fresh air or to get away from the rest of the people in the unit. But they took her advice. For the next three days they didn't leave the house at all.

It was well that the unit took the additional precaution. The noise of fighting grew heavier and more persistent. The center of a battle seemed to be growing closer. Gunships, helicopters armed with rockets and machine guns, spewed lead all afternoon on NVA positions between the ARVN compound and the large lovely Catholic cathedral.

By 5:30, just as the team's thoughts were turning toward their second rationed meal for the day, artillery suddenly exploded nearby, rocking the house and shattering more windows. They were no sooner in the bunker than they heard Chi Hai calling for them. Keefer clambered out of the shelter and ran to the door to let her and the two orphan girls who live with her into the house and down into the bomb shelter. It was a crowded, frightened group who sat in the dark bunker for three hours as round after round of artillery smashed about their house.

Sometime after eight o'clock, when silence had filtered down over the area, the fellows crawled out and slept on the floor about the hole of the shelter. The girls spent the whole night sitting on wooden chairs in the bunker. For June, that night was an ugly thing that went on and on and on. Only the words of the psalmist and memory of friendship with particular Vietnamese sustained her, kept her from cursing her plight, and thus wiping out her ministry of the past year.

One such close friendship was with Co Tuyen, the Vietnamese home extension worker in Hue. She was a trained home economist who had studied in the States. June and Co Tuyen teamed up for numerous programs. Co Tuyen occasionally came to the Training Center to give talks to June's classes or take the students out to the villages to show them some of the home improvement work being done at that level. Other times June would accompany Co Tuyen on visits to the 4-T clubs.

"Co Tuyen would ask for suggestions," June once wrote, "but what she really needed was just recognition for the hard work in a program she was carrying. She did not receive this recognition from other people or places. She looked to me for that approval.

73

"I also was able to help Co Tuyen with the training classes for her workers. As we sat together I learned much from her too as she explained more fully the nature of the work being conducted in the many villages. As we talked together I would become so excited about the work I would forget that I was an American and she a Vietnamese."

The fellows rose early the morning of their first week to assess the damage hurled on them the night before. All the windows were knocked out and the drapes blown down. Three six-to-eight-inch holes gaped in the east living-room wall facing the street. Cracks jagged across many of the walls. Bricks, plaster, cement, and glass covered the furniture and floors. Flying shrapnel had also shattered the windshield of one of the three VNCS cars parked in the driveway. The power plant was burning, as well as several houses behind June's house.

But their house was still standing. And they were unharmed. It should have been enough to cause great rejoicing. But the week had taken its toll. And as June sat in the bunker listening to the whisper of the broom across the floor overhead she wanted to do nothing, absolutely nothing—but cry.

A week. How long is a week? For some a few bright hours of vacation stolen from months and months of gray work. For others a blur of rapid time passing in fruitful work. A week—that week in

Hue—for June was a nightmare of hours upon hours upon hours of waiting, of watching and waiting. Never had a week fallen such terrible lengths. And a new week was beginning.

NVA snipers now lodged in the houses across the street from June's. Other NVA again trotted up and down the street. With the gaping holes in the living room the team took further precaution.

"We'll have to stay in the hallway and the bunker."

The extreme confinement was an additional burden but no one groaned nor argued the point. They stacked cushions and pillows in the bunker—just in case they would have to spend another night there. They might at least attempt to make it a mite more comfortable.

And that was the day's work. But it was still early morning. And the emptiness of waiting lay ahead of them. Some read, many tried sleeping, a few played card games, and one or two of the fellows could not resist the temptation to take "emergency" peeks out of the holes in the living-room wall to return with reports of the activity in the streets, or the lack of it.

The first week passed. In general, the seven team members had kept in as good spirits as possible. Except for a touch of diarrhea, their health had been good. Food and water, under strict rationing, was holding out. They had each lost about ten pounds.

Thatched villages snuggled along the coast.

When night drifted down, the team again repeated together the Twenty-third Psalm. "He leadeth me beside the still waters. . . ." Some divine quietness entered June as the lips of her heart phrased the words. The realization that life was very short and that what she had done day by day in Vietnam was important drifted through her mind. If she lived, she must see this experience as not just a moment of suffering and fear but as part of her total life. If she lived . . . ?

She had received a new sense of what the refugee experienced as she saw them carry their packs of things through the streets, not knowing where they fled. Or the mothers and older children carrying in a litter a wounded member of their family up the street to the hospital. And seeing the same people come back down the street a few days later with a blanket draped over a still body. Life had ended. . . . It had not yet ended for her. "I will fear no evil," June thought, "for thou art with me. . . ."

Tanks fired all morning the eighth day. At times the din was so great that the volunteers thought all the VC or NVA must surely have been driven into their section of the city and were making one last heroic effort to withstand the American and ARVN onslaught. But during occasional lulls, they could hear the heavy bombing and rocketing in the direction of the Citadel. By midmorning they no longer saw NVA men at their posts or on the streets.

The day's first meal—at eleven o'clock—was two figs and three tablespoons of juice. For the second day the seven VNCSers kept themselves to the hallway and the bunker. (The two Vietnamese orphan girls were still with them though June's cook had left the house earlier in the morning.) All of them had sore teeth, having had no water to spare for days to brush them. The smell of unwashed bodies was embarrassingly heavy. And again for the second day all conversation was conducted in whispers.

Yet, in spite of the growing discomforts of the last days, a hint of hope grew as the eighth day died. None of the unit could have put into words a certain faint whisper from Providence that quickened the pulse, that kindled a spirit of expectancy. Perhaps their crucible at Hue was about to end.

"Let's eat Aunt Gertie's nuts," Sandoz said as he volunteered a tin of nuts an aunt had sent him for June to use in a cake.

"And open one of those tins of Spam."

"But slice it thin," June said, a light caution against any premature celebrations.

"When I get out of here, I'm gonna stand under a shower for hours and sing," Kooker whispered exaltedly. Everybody muffled his laughter, well aware that they were not yet "out of here," but the thought of standing in stingingly clean water was a delight and some laughed again—just to think of it.

Dusk came and then the darkness and then the long hours of the night but nothing had happened. No one had thrown wide the door for them to freedom. No one had dropped by the house to tell them it was safe, that they could return to the classrooms and fields and hamlets, they they could again go about their ministries. But still hope rose, though none spoke of it.

And that night at prayers the words of the psalmist broke through June's numb walls of despair and fear: "Surely goodness and mercy shall follow me. . . . And I shall dwell in the house of the Lord. . . ."

It was a thought she could go quietly to sleep on, though an occasional scream of artillery tore a hole in the night.

Before June could sleep her mind was again casting up some memories to be lived through. They flowed in and out with unfulfilled schemes of months past, of future plans for new programs at the Center. Snatches of past conversations returned to mind. Faces and experiences of people she had not thought of or worked with for months drifted back again. One such person was a teacher at the school.

The Vietnamese director came to her suddenly one day and announced that a certain teacher would have to be fired. He had TB. June's first response was to agree, if that were truly the case. Later she thought differently about the matter and urged that the

79

When will gentleness return to the village, to the boys and their ox?

teacher be given the chance to take another TB test.

"The discussion went on for weeks," June wrote. "I noticed that the Vietnamese director was upset and getting more people involved. And by this time the teacher was discouraged and fearful of losing his job, which meant so much to him.

"Finally, we got him off to the hospital for tests and we made the staff hold off firing him or hiring a replacement. When he came back, his tests showed that he was clean.

"Here is what we found out: While at the university he had contracted tuberculosis. Having to drop out of his classes, he took a treatment for TB at the hospital. After being released, he came to us at the Center as a teacher. Another of our staff members, who wanted to get one of his relatives into a teaching position, happened to know of this fellow's TB record. He used it as a way of getting him off the staff.

"This made me angry, particularly because the teacher who once had TB was not a Christian and the ones plotting against him were Christian. It was a tense situation to work through. But finally we got it settled."

Life took on new meaning for the young teacher. He expressed in his own way gratitude to June for her having taken an interest in his problem and helping him through it. He even began attending Bible knowledge classes at the Training Center. The

An evening spent at June Sauder's house with Vietnamese university students. The American in the foreground is Paul Kennel.

last June saw him before Tet he was happily going about his teaching assignment at the Center. He seemed to have found again a sense of direction.

June wanted to live out at the Training Center or at one of the refugee centers instead of seven to ten kilometers off in Hue.

"I want to live out there so desperately, but because we are working in a very insecure area, this is impossible. The village chief instructed us never to be out after five o'clock and we learned from various incidents that this was wise counsel.

"So we try to be satisfied with living in town, though our work is out in the villages. There is no use crying over the situation. Instead, we are making friends in town, particularly with a number of university students.

"They come to our house to visit, to practice English, to learn about America. We learn about Vietnam and practice our Vietnamese. We have had a number of parties. I enjoyed the one at Christmas-time, especially when we sat together singing carols. To many of them it was a new custom."

"Goodness and mercy shall follow me. . . ." Sleep came gently, and June relaxed deeply into it on her mattress on the bathroom floor. It would be her last night in Hue.

6.

Joy Comes in the Morning
(The Escape on the Ninth Day)

The morning of the ninth day was tranquil. Mist-shrouded skies hung heavily in the city's treetops. The watchers in the house on Nguyen Hue Street looked out on a desolate scene of rubble. The Catholic school and cathedral were crumbled nearly beyond recognition. The power plant, a smoldering heap. Other large buildings and many houses were leveled or had sections of walls or roofs blasted away. The NVA were not at their posts; none moved in the streets. It was Thursday, February 8.

"I knew they'd be gone."

"Saw twenty-five heading out of town late last night."

"And sometime after midnight I was up and saw another two dozen NVAs running out of town. They weren't carrying their packs and some of them had torn uniforms. I knew that if they were running off without their packs, they must be leaving town."

Later that morning the team could hear Vietnamese conversing together somewhere down the streets. They saw children playing among the rubble. It was a good sign. The civilians were moving back into the city.

"I wonder how long we should wait before we take a look around?"

"Relax, man, we could still be here awhile."

"I think we'd better clean up some more of the dirt in the house. It'll give us something to do."

"Yeah, it'll help pass the time and keep our minds on something else."

Following a leisurely eleven o'clock breakfast of prunes only, the team decided to wile some time away by playing cards. From time to time someone would go to the window, hopeful that something was happening. None of them knew what to expect; aside from the one conversation three of the fellows had four days ago with the two Americans who operated the television station, the team had made no contact with the outside world. Who of their American friends in Hue would think that the VNCSers were still in their headquarters? Had their Saigon directors given them up for dead?

"Listen!"

Everyone stopped shuffling his cards.

"I hear American voices!"

Several of the fellows ran to the door and listened carefully, breathless with excitement.

"FORWARD!"

"It's the marines! It's gotta be!"

But still they could not see them. Nevertheless, each person rushed about the house grabbing up personal items. Sandoz ran to the safe and emptied its contents into a briefcase.

"I see 'em!" Someone shouted from the door. "U.S. marines! Hundreds of them!"

Rarely were Americans so glad to see U.S. marines as were the seven VNCS volunteers, pacifists or no pacifists.

Kennel waved to the first marine slipping up the street along courtyard walls and between rows of trees. He was noticed.

"You speak English?" the marine yelled across the street.

"Yeah! We're Americans!"

"Get down to the corner!"

"Let's go, gang," Kennel called to the others.

But just as they were about to cross the street and run to the corner another whole contingent of marines on foot swung into view, rifles in the ready. For a moment, the VNCSers were confused. Should they attempt a dash for the other side, getting in front of the marines jogging up the street? Might they be mistaken as fleeing from instead of running for the marines' protection?

"You better get outa there! You better get outa there!" The first marine's yells set them running. It seemed a strangely insistent command, almost humorously so, to the unit darting across the street. After waiting eight and a half days, it was not immediately apparent why the sudden rush!

"Who are you?" marines asked brusquely.

"We're with Vietnam Christian Service."

"How long you been in there?" They motioned toward the house, their eyes scanning other buildings for snipers.

"Eight and a half days!"

"My God! And you're still alive!"

"Yeah! It's a miracle!"

"It's hell! Get on down to that house on the corner. We'll call a vehicle from MACV to pick you up."

During the fifteen minutes they waited for the lift, the VNCSers saw the leathernecks attempt to dig out the elusive but stubborn Viet Cong.

Going from house to house, the marines called out at the doors for the people to come out. If no one came to unlock the door, they either kicked it open or sprayed it with machine gun fire, occasionally tossing a hand grenade into the house. If the marines received as much as one shot from a house they returned heavy fire, unable to tell who were VC or NVA, since many had slipped into civilian dress.

June turned away, finding the mop-up operations impossible to watch. She was too relieved to be rescued herself to acknowledge the horror of the hunt —until some injured Vietnamese civilians came by— people who had not come out of their homes quickly enough, people who probably had not understood the Americans' commands in garbled Vietnamese. It struck her savagely, then. She was alive but all about her others—Vietnamese and Americans—were getting killed.

A pickup truck carried June and her colleagues to the MACV compound. On the way it dodged huge holes freshly blown out of the paved street, decomposing bodies of civilians and soldiers slumped where they had fallen in desperate leaps to escape, and a tangle of downed wires, splintered trees, and stranded vehicles.

From the noise of the shelling and bombing taking place during the past eight and one-half days, and from the views they could glimpse from their own windows during that time, the team expected to see heavy destruction. But none was prepared for the view about them as they joggled on the truck en route to the compound. They were speechless, staring with unbelieving eyes at the massive spread of ruin and devastation. House after house after house, shops, schools, and other buildings had great holes blown through them, or most of their walls were only heaps of crumbled stones and plaster; roofs were smashed into gutted buildings. The huge bridge crossing the Perfume River was broken in the middle.

It was a scene from a World War II movie. And over it all the red-and-blue flag of the Viet Cong fluttered gently.

Hue was like a scene in a World War II movie.

At the MACV compound, intelligence officers were not a little amazed to see seven Americans, sound and healthy, walk into their offices. The officers took the VNCSers to the chapel and offered them cigarettes. Finding themselves with a bunch of nonsmokers on their hands, the officers in a desperate but silly attempt to be congenial offered June and her team candy.

Intelligence questioned them for a brief time, all the while kicking out a swarm of American reporters who kept invading the room for a scoop.

Here the VNCS team learned that the International Voluntary Service team at Hue were missing, that several of the USAID people were killed and a few still missing, and that the German medical team had been captured. Just before leaving MACV compound, a USAID person came up to June. He was carrying Tom's passport.

"Have you seen or heard anything of him?"

Oh! no, God! She prayed silently.

"He's missing," the man said, anticipating the question of June's frightened eyes.

She had steeled herself for the truth of such words to break over her; but yet when they came, something turned to water inside her and bits of renewed courage flowed away. The joy of her own escape fell under a long gray shadow. Oh! God, keep him safe!

Another truck whipped them off to a landing ramp on the Perfume River. No air traffic was running because of bad weather. But a landing craft, off-loading ammunition at the ramp, would be returning to Danang.

During the two-hour wait, the VNCSers were swamped with questions from news reporters for AP, CBS-TV, *Time* Magazine, *Washington Post*, and others. Mortar fire from VC broke up the news interviews as everyone scrambled for cover.

Finally, they boarded the landing craft for the seven-hour ride to Danang. Nearly a hundred marines were on board, some wounded and a few dead. Eight patrol boats accompanied the craft.

The first hour was smooth riding, as the boat dropped down the Perfume River. But as it broke out into the open South China Sea, fifteen-foot waves rolled the vessel sickeningly. June and Pauline were invited into the captain's quarters; even so, they both became miserably seasick.

As June lay rolling and lurching in a chair her mind returned to the morning's escape from the house into the protection of the marines. Everything had happened quickly; there was no time for thoughts, only action. But now, as she reflected on the incident, she found that she did have some feelings about leaving her Vietnamese colleagues and accepting the protection of the military. She was an American civilian, a Christian pacifist, a Mennonite. She worked with an organization which struggled to keep clear its identity as being an agency of Christian compassion, separate from the American military presence in Vietnam.

It was a confusing situation but there was quietness in June's conscience. The marines did not invade Hue to rescue her VNCS team. The volunteers simply took advantage of the arrival of the marines as a time to escape. June was grateful for the fact that during the whole time, from the moment they ran from her house to their arrival at the landing ramp on the river, no shots had been fired for her or her team's protection.

A message had been radioed ahead so that a USAID official met the boat at Danang. The team was taken to a naval billet for the night. The first warm shower in nine days, the smell of fresh sheets, the quiet soft skies overhead—it was all a little too much too suddenly for June, after a nine-day siege in hell. For once it was safe enough to let go inside. "Surely goodness and mercy shall follow me. . . ." She smiled and wept and drifted into sleep.

In the morning, Jerry Sandoz walked over to Roy Josephsen's house, a Christian and Missionary Alliance missionary. They praised God at seeing Sandoz; their Vietnamese colleagues were equally amazed. "Hey, you're supposed to be dead!" they said.

Roy and Sandoz returned to the billet to take all the people to the Josephsens' home for breakfast. Later the unit picked out some clothing for themselves from the bundles of relief commodities held in storage. For once, they were the needy victims of war, refugees fleeing with only the clothes on their backs.

After several unsuccessful attempts, Kennel was able to get a telephone message through to the Vietnam Christian Service headquarters in Saigon. The administrators there had nearly despaired of getting any good news after such a long interval. They had made inquiries through the United States embassy several times each day about personnel from whom they had not heard. As the days passed, they had nearly become resigned to their fears that their unit in Hue was killed.

Saigon asked the Hue unit to come down immediately. Tomorrow would be the earliest flight. That very afternoon, when the team wanted to do nothing but rest, they received a message to come to the USAID compound for security. A rocket attack was expected. The night was spent on cots, and some of the old tenseness returned to June, who took medication to help relax.

Shortly after noon the next day—Saturday, February 10—the Hue VNCSers boarded a plane for Saigon.

"Of course everyone in Saigon was mighty glad to see us," June recounted on a tape recording she made for her parents after she arrived in Saigon. "They just about had given us up as dead and figured they would never see us again. It was almost harder for them to accept the fact that we were alive and well than the fact that we were missing and would never be seen again. So it was quite a time of rejoicing. All the other units had been accounted for and everyone was well. Not one member was hurt; all were safe.

"Sunday morning we talked with William Snyder and Atlee Beechy, here on an administrative visit from the States. They assured us that we would not have to make any major decisions at this time. What we all needed was some rest. We were not to worry about the future."

A few days later June left with the VNCS wives and children, who were being evacuated to Penang Island, Malaysia. She was to take a month's holiday before making any decisions about her future assignment. It was fairly obvious that Hue was so completely destroyed that there was little question about her returning there for domestic science assistance. Where else? It didn't matter just now.

As far as it is possible to know, all the other American houses in Hue were entered by the Viet Cong or the North Vietnamese Army. The VC and NVA were moving up and down the street by June's house. They must have known that Americans lived there—with three American vehicles parked out front. Why didn't they enter June's house?

"It was the hand of God protecting us," Paul Kennel declared before his administrators in Saigon.

"It truly was a modern-day miracle," several of the other fellows said.

"It might have been our association with the Training Center and the Vietnamese Protestant Church," Jerry Sandoz wrote. "They probably know that we never carried any weapons."

William T. Snyder, executive secretary of MCC, who was in Saigon on an administrative visit at the time of the Tet offensive wrote, "Paul Kennel was right in stating that God delivered them. But I suspect that they were spared because of the great value placed on the Hue project by the local Vietnamese people since its beginning.

"The World Relief Commission project, to which VNCS personnel were loaned, has brought improved agriculture to the area through a demonstration farm and better education through a school project. The Viet Cong, who have been active near the projects during the past several years, never molested the pigs, poultry, or property. I believe that the value of the project to the people and the importance of the work the team was doing, plus the fact that they went unarmed and attempted to stay clear of any political involvement, may have been key factors in this miracle at Hue.

"As we now rejoice in the news from Hue, we are saddened by the deaths of six Christian and Missionary Alliance missionaries at Banmethuot, which is the same location from which Daniel Gerber and two others were abducted seven years ago."

The mind is confused and there is no easy answer. Why were some Christian workers killed and others unmolested? It is an unanswerable bafflement, whose key lies with God. But it must be said that the VNCS team were not more dedicated than the C & MA team—they might even have been less. Given any other situation and location, the Viet Cong might not have understood the VNCS and would have then captured or killed them.

"During those days we had many questions as to whether or not we would ever get out," June wrote later. "We did not discuss it much because we realized that we were there for a long stay and that we had to make the best of it. We would have to trust our friends and those outside for help and prayers.

"We were all very glad to get out, but it's hard to explain how an experience that is so very frightening can be so sweet and have such meaning. Now that I am away from the experience I find that it has done something to me. It has given me a new realization of what life is all about, and that each day is so important."

During her vacation, it became evident to June that she should not think of returning to any other assignment in Vietnam. In Hue she was well known. In other villages she would be a stranger. And it was not the time to be moving as a stranger among new villages.

"For me I find it very difficult to accept some of the things that happened and to realize that I cannot go back to the situation where I was. Work was going well and everything was seemingly under control at the Training Center. We were beginning to see things happen in our work. Now suddenly to have it all wiped out—it is hard to accept. I now see how little I understood the stamina of my fellow Vietnamese colleagues. How they kept their heads high and kept going even when the work of their hands had crumbled about them for the second time or more!"

June returned to her home near Lancaster, Pennsylvania, the first of April for a few months' rest and rehabilitation. During this time she learned of the release of the two Americans captured by the Viet Cong in Hue. Sandra Johnson of International Voluntary Service and Dr. Marjorie Nelson of American Friends Service Committee had spent 52 days with members of the National Liberation Front in a prison camp in the mountains. Later they were led to a spot north of Hue. Their captors set them free, pointing to Highway I. June rejoiced to learn of their release. She was thankful that she was spared such experiences, kind though the IVS captors were.

During the last week of July, June left for Brazil

Children at the school for refugee children eat bread during a snack and proudly wear Vietnamese outfits made in U.S. by various church groups.

to begin a new assignment under Mennonite Central Committee. At that time she said, "I am convinced more than ever that God uses ordinary people in His work. I had always looked at people for whom God did miracles or through whom He worked in extraordinary ways as people who were perfect. But I find this is not true. God doesn't ask us to be perfect before we serve Him. Anyone thoroughly committed to Him, God uses—each in some small way."

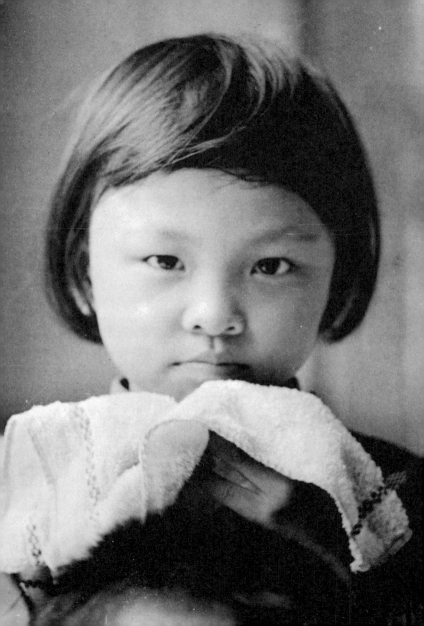

7.

A Phoenix for Hue
(Post-Tet Discoveries)

Three weeks after the seven Vietnam Christian Service volunteers fled Hue, two of the fellows returned. Paul Kennel and Ken Keefer not only wanted to discover the extent of the damage to their houses and the Training Center but to also assess the refugee situation and learn how their own Vietnamese colleagues fared during the offensive.

At June's house they found her cook living in and watching over the place. June's house sustained greater damage from near hits of artillery than did the fellows' house or the Hochstetler house. All the furnishings and June's personal effects, however, were safe. At the other two houses, however, looters had ransacked the rooms, closets, and drawers, carrying off anything of value. Mattresses, clothing, cameras, radio were plundered. Even the stove, refrigerator, and washing machine had been lugged off from one of the houses. It was the same story with many of the homes of Vietnamese neighbors and friends.

Following the Tet offensive, Ken Keefer returned to inspect June's house.

"But who looted?" the fellows asked, though they knew the answer to their own question.

Repeatedly they were told that when the marines came into the city they carried off with them anything portable and of value. It was a selective looting, but looting none the less, and mild compared to the activities of the ARVN soldiers when they eventually returned to the city.

And repeatedly Kennel and Keefer were told by the Vietnamese in Hue, "If this is what the United States is and if this is what the South Vietnamese government is, we don't want anything to do with it. The NVA were polite. They came in, asked questions, and paid for their food. Maybe it wasn't South Vietnamese currency but it was at least money."

"But what about the massacre?" the fellows might have asked. Near the Training Center their friends had pointed out a mass grave in which, it was rumored, more than 500 people were buried.

"During the first days the North Vietnamese had everything under their control. It was only later that the Viet Cong began kidnapping and murdering." Or so it was reported.

After seeing and hearing about the widespread looting which took place, the fellows were sure that the VNCS warehouse could hardly have been missed. But they found the warehouse locked and more than 2,000 bags of bulgar wheat and cornmeal untouched. Everything was still there—except a few pieces of

Paul Kennel inspects the Tet offensive damage to the office of the Training Center.

clothing. Apparently someone had knocked open the lock, helped himself to a few shirts and a pair of trousers from the bundles of relief clothing stored there, and left again, kindly locking up the warehouse after him!

None of the three VNCS vehicles had been stolen or irreparably damaged. Only three of the ten 55-gallon drums of gasoline stored in the fellows' garage had been used, apparently by the marines.

Everything was on hand—vehicles, gasoline, food— and there were thousands of needy refugees everywhere Kennel and Keefer turned. The fellows went to work immediately, distributing food and clothing to refugees in several of the crowded camps receiving no help from the government. They initiated a bread-feeding program, bringing up flour supplies on hired junks from Danang.

At the Training Center, outside Hue, the fellows found the school and farm buildings in good shape. But all the livestock was stolen, as well as some sewing machines and carpentry and mechanic tools.

"The VC stole the pigs, chickens, and the cows," Kennel wrote, "but they did not hurt the people who were taking care of the pigs, chickens, and cows, even though they knew that they worked for us Americans."

Not one Vietnamese person associated with the Training Center program was killed or injured during the Tet offensive. The local Protestant church, the

The Viet Cong had dug a tunnel through the chicken house at the Training Center.

youth group, and those closely associated with the World Relief Commission, which sponsors the Training Center, were not seriously molested or intimidated by the Viet Cong. It was providential.

Finding their Vietnamese co-workers alive and ready to build again was a joyous experience for Kennel and Keefer. It was also humbling. For they knew that they, as well as each member of the team —Vietnamese and American alike—had been allotted a few more years of life for some purpose. Now to be diligent, to be faithful to that trust.

June Sauder

Omar Eby

The Author

Born in Hagerstown, Md., in 1935, Omar Eby was educated at Eastern Mennonite College, Harrisonburg, Va. After graduating with a BA degree, he taught English for three years as a missionary to Somalia, the locale for *Sense and Insense* of which he is author.

Upon returning to the States, Mr. Eby taught at the Lancaster Mennonite High School, Lancaster, Pa., before taking his MA degree from the School of Journalism, Syracuse University, Syracuse, N.Y. During two of the several years he edited the *Missionary Messenger*, the official publication of the Eastern Mennonite Board of Missions and Charities, Salunga, Pa., he taught English and journalism at Eastern Mennonite College.

He has traveled in Africa, Europe, and the Middle East. Returning from a second teaching assignment in Africa— this time in Tanzania—he assumed responsibilities as Secretary of Information Services for Mennonite Central Committee, Akron, Pa.

Mr. Eby is married to Anna Kathryn Shenk, who was born and reared in Tanzania, being the daughter of missionaries. The Ebys make their home in Lancaster, Pa.

He is author of *A Whisper in a Dry Land*.